Hollywood
AT HOME

NOSCAR
AWARD
PAUL NEWMA

Hollywood AT HOME

A Family Album 1950-1965

Photographs by Sid Avery

Text by Richard Schickel

Crown Publishers, Inc.
New York

Published by Crown Publishers, Inc., 201 East 50th Street, New York, New York 10022.
Member of the Crown Publishing Group

CROWN is a trademark of Crown Publishers, Inc.

Manufactured in Japan

Library of Congress Cataloging-in-Publication Data
Avery, Sid.
Hollywood at home: a family album, 1950–1965 / photographs by Sid Avery; text by Richard Schickel.—1st ed.
p. cm.
1. Motion picture actors and actresses—United States—Portraits.
2. Television personalities—United States—Portraits.
3. Entertainers—United States—Portraits. I. Schickel, Richard.
II. Title.
PN1998.2.A85 1990 89-71211
CIP

ISBN 0-517-57696-1

Book design by Linda Kocur

10 9 8 7 6 5 4 3 2 1

First Edition

To my parents for making their home in the U.S.A. and California in particular.

To my Uncle Max for being my teacher, mentor, and friend.

To Diana my love, for everything.

—S.A.

ACKNOWLEDGMENTS

I am indebted to my son Ronald for preparing the prints and keeping me organized.

I am especially grateful to the following for their continued assistance and consultation in the preparations of this book: Alan Stamm, Robert Duffy, Jean Sapin.

To Eero Cooke, Douglas Davis, Graham Driscoll, and Bill Rolf for their help and friendship.

Many thanks to Peter Miller for his persistance and unbounded energy on my behalf.

—S.A.

Special thanks go to our editor Gail Kinn for her patience and her help in making this book work out. To Linda Kocur for her superb design sensibility; and to Ken Sansone and David Groff for their many contributions.

...Better Than Ever

SID AVERY'S HOLLYWOOD

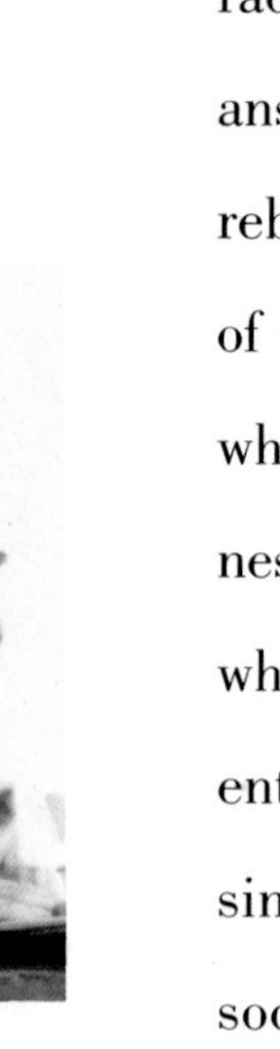

In Sid Avery's portraits of Hollywood in the 1950s, its citizens mime normalcy. They diaper a baby, fry an egg, play charades, wash their cars. Beloved screen veterans, members of a threatened hierarchy; young rebels challenging them with their new ways of performing, of being; television performers whose medium was the menace to show business as usual. The serenity and seemliness with which all of them face the camera in this, the entertainment industry's most chaotic moment since the advent of sound films, strikes the social historian—not to mention the movie critic—with a strange and occasionally poignant force. Some variant on this question keeps recurring as one turns these pages: Why are these people smiling?

Even when they are caught in public, entering a theater or eating in a restaurant, they are for the most part decorous in dress and manner. They look more like anonymous suburbanites out for a modest night on the town than famous folk preening their fine feathers. And when they are glimpsed at work, they are shown to be sober and democratic. They do not put on airs, and neither do they sulk. They relate pleasantly to their less favored colleagues, show not the least sign of "artistic temperament." Oh, yes, every once in a while someone like Debbie Reynolds is caught kicking up her heels, or someone like Marlon Brando or James Dean seems to be signaling silent, though not necessarily permanent (or even ill-spirited), withdrawal from accustomed mannerliness. But even that doesn't matter deeply. They're here, aren't they? Doing the necessary, making themselves available to the camera, submitting to the then current conventions of celebrity self-exhibition. This superficial calm permitted the original readers of these images to reflect as comfortably on their younger subjects as they did on the more settled elders: Sid Avery also portrayed a certain waywardness as a predictable part of growing up. These kids will settle down, won't they? Of course they will. Everybody does eventually.

At the time we read no intimations of tragedy, or even the possibility of future disappointments, into any of these images. Our tendency in those days was to regard such thoughts as unworthy of us. For like these favored show folk, the rest of us ordinary citizens of the American 1950s were busy miming normalcy, too. It was expected of us. A depression had been survived, a war had been fought, and now everything was supposed to be coming out all right. Was going to come out all right. Public doubt on that point was discouraged; private anxieties about it were suppressed. What we were supposed to do was fold hands and believe. Get married. Have 2.3 children. Work for a corporation offering good fringe benefits. Buy a house in the suburbs. Go to church. Take PTA seriously. Send the kids to college. Travelgolfcollectputter. Retire contentedly. Die quietly. It was an agreeable, undramatic, yet, in these suddenly prosperous times, entirely plausible scenario.

There was much wishful thinking in this behavior and no small amount of willful innocence as well. For—as the entertainment industry, beset by the forces of radical change, had good reason to know—there was something abnormal about fifties normalcy. At best, the word refers us, in any period, to nothing more than a temporarily agreed-upon consensus about what the culturally dominant middle class believes to constitute the good—or at least respectable—life for its members and its aspirants. But in this decade that consensus seemed broader, easier to define, and more sternly enforced than ever, and it evoked fewer questions, protests, alternatives.

Yet everyone also knows that no matter how all-encompassing it appears to be, millions are inevitably excluded from any such consensus—or quietly exclude themselves from it. What was clear to a relatively small number of social commentators at the time now appears a truism to all of us as we look back upon this decade: The great fifties consensus was in the largest sense a fraud or, at best, a kind of metafiction. On most important matters—the relationships between the races, sexes, classes, and generations, for example—it grotesquely, even tragically, misrepresented reality.

In my case, fifties normalcy, especially as the concept was amplified (and, in the process, further distorted) through the mass media of the time, cannot be characterized as a full representation of reality. Or as a very interesting or dramatically compelling representation

of it. As with all fictions, one was free not to buy it. One was not even obliged to read its reviews. But the mass media did buy it and sell it, to the exclusion of all the alternative realities. And we, the great audience, bought it from the movies and the magazines and the broadcasters. We also did our best to resell it, to our sometimes dubious selves and then to each other.

The pictures in this book were made as part of that process. They represented Hollywood as it wanted to see itself and to be seen by outsiders at this troubled time in its history: securely functioning and apparently conducting its business as usual. They also represented Hollywood as the editors of certain mass magazines (mostly the most bourgeois of them all, the *Saturday Evening Post*) believed their readers wanted to see it—as a community of stable, good-natured types not essentially different from those one might find gathered in other less exotic venues, working at other less glamorous trades. Many of these images were also, frankly, representations of our own dreams of success as the atmosphere of the fifties formed those dreams. This is how we would live, this is how we would behave, if fortune smiled upon us: in a kind of suburbia raised to flash point, a place where the sun always shined, the kids were always happy, and we could modestly, tastefully indulge our material fantasies—for a swell car, a swimming pool, maybe even an oceangoing sailboat.

I have no doubt that as they were originally published (discreetly, one or two at a time, accompanying rather bland profiles of well-known show biz personalities), these photographs functioned just as the editors who commissioned them, and the press agents who helped arrange some of them, hoped they would—reassuring readers that these starry creatures were just folks. But we do not see them that way, not in this book. Seen for the first time as a group, after the passage of three and four decades, they transcend their original context, becoming both a vivid impressionistic history of a period in which our popular culture was quietly but permanently revolutionized and, still more interesting, a sly and often subversive comment on the very values the pictures were supposed to perpetuate.

To produce pictures of this kind is an enviable achievement. Here is a remarkable body of work that at the time of its creation satisfied the bland expectations of its subjects and clients and yet survives to engage our own more knowing (perhaps more cynical, certainly more ironic) eye. It has been attained, I think, because despite the journalistic occasions that called forth his commissions, Sid Avery did not conceive of himself as a journalist, a smash-and-grab recorder of events in progress. By which I do not mean to imply that he imagined himself as an artist in the fullest sense of the word, either—he is too modest and unpretentious to claim a self-definition I know he would regard as self-inflating.

When he began making these pictures—a young man with a young family to support, living back in his hometown and resuming his career after World War Two service in army photographic units, which had helped him to hone his professional skills—I believe Sid Avery saw himself primarily as an illustrator in much the same sense as painters like Norman Rockwell and others whose work had for so long appeared on the covers and in the pages of magazines like the *Post*. This supposition is based in part on what I know about the rest of his life and career and in part on the evidence supplied by the photographs themselves.

The largest formative influence on his work was certainly that of an uncle named Max Tatch, a landscape and architectural photographer who achieved no fame, but whose images of Los Angeles in the thirties and forties, to judge by the few examples that still exist, had the kind of formal perfection—and mysteriously haunting resonance—one associates with Atget's images of turn-of-the-century Paris. Tatch became Sid Avery's mentor when, during adolescence, Avery began to take an interest in photography. And even though their subject matter could not be more disparate, one sees the uncle's influence in the careful, often elegant way his nephew composed and lit his photographs. The studio work Avery did before the war, the pictures he took when he was off-duty during it (most of his work was of a highly technical nature), the career he went on to after the period covered by this book, when he worked in advertising, first as a photographer, then as a producer-director of television commercials, all propose a sensibility less attuned to the hand-held candor of photojournalism than to the technical polish and thought-out compositional strength of illustration.

But even if one knew nothing of Avery's history, one would sense, from the most superficial glance at the pictures gathered here, his affinity with the latter tradition. His aim, like that of all illustrators, was to try to summarize his subject in a single richly detailed image, one in which the subject's immediate situation—the environment in which we discover him—deepens our understanding of the larger contexts shaping his life. In the case of a famous person, this also includes his sense of what our expectations of him may be. Photography of this kind does not, of course, give us the whole story of a life—what single image, painted or photographed, possibly can? At its best, though, it can offer a very telling anecdote. And, inferentially, it can also tell us much about the historical moment in which a picture, or a set of pictures, was made.

We are not talking simple realism here. We are talking of a carefully heightened, and somewhat stylized, realism, something that results from, say, a slight improvement in the natural light of a scene, or the elimination, through careful framing, of the irrelevant or distracting detail, or a murmured suggestion of a bit of action or a change of expression to the subject. In other words, we are talking about a subtle reshaping of reality that permits the photographer to impose his own interpretative comment on what at first glance appears to be a rather ordinary scene.

The method of work that in large measure shaped the manner of Sid Avery's photographs was dictated in part by certain traditions that had long governed the relationship between photographer and celebrity subjects in the Hollywood of the fifties. Some of these had grown out of this immutable fact: Most performers dislike and distrust the still camera. This may seem odd, considering the narcissism that is so often a large part of their natures. But remember that what they are usually selling is not repose, but animation, a full range of expression, movement, and vocal qualities—all of which the still photograph denies them. Remember, too, that a star at work in front of a motion picture or television camera is the most cosseted of creatures, the leading participant in the process of processing his image for public consumption. His enemy in both situations is the nasty surprise, the sneak attack on *amour-propre*. This was particularly true in the 1950s, the dawn of the paparazzi age, when a new breed of photographer was beginning to lurk at the corner of the celebrity's eyeline, hoping to catch him unaware, with his image askew.

Thus, a still photographer, especially one invading a star's home and as often as not requiring his family's participation in the photographic rite, had to do what he could to assuage a vast anxiety that was often expressed as anger and impatience. And that inevitably included making a careful show of arranging the scene, lighting it with something like the consideration that goes into lighting a movie scene, keeping the poses he proposed within the star's sense of self and image, and generally making a fuss over his subject. The point, of course, was to make his little shoot resemble as much as possible a movie or television shoot, where everything was arranged to make the performer feel not merely comfortable, but in control of his situation—at least to the extent that he is able to avoid thoughtless exploitation.

A large factor in creating this trusting atmosphere was the photographer's sense of what his subject and his peers had permitted in the past. It was true that in this new age of television (later in the decade the magazines were competing against TV shows like *Person to Person,* in which celebrities gave guided tours of their homes for Edward R. Murrow and his cameras) somewhat greater intimacy than had been permitted previously was tolerated. Before, the only lensmen invited into a star's home were docile studio employees. It was also true that all concerned were under pressure to provide a certain novelty of pose and situation, something that would arrest the reader's ever-impatient and increasingly distracted eye. For this was the beginning of the image explosion.

But these were, after all, the fifties. We had not yet arrived at that persistent prurience that now pertains in celebrity journalism. And no one—other than the scandal-mongering *Confidential* and its clones—wanted to revert to the equally problematic days of the 1920s, when Hollywood imagery tended to stress the disparities between stars and audience. In that time displays of wealth, idleness, and peculiar tastes in everything from interior design to hairstyles were regularly encountered in the newspapers and magazines. They titillated, but they also distanced—and were no help at all in convincing the public that the occasional highly publicized Hollywood scandal was to be regarded as an anomaly, not the norm. By the early thirties (coincident with the arrival of sound films, which had a powerfully democratizing effect on both screen content and star imagery) the studios and the press had conspired to create quite a different, more generally acceptable publicity convention: Hollywood as small town, Hollywood as exemplar of traditional American virtues, which became one of the most enduring conceits of popular jour-

nalism. It had served everyone very well, surviving the onslaughts of the candid cameramen with their light equipment and fast films that enabled them to go everywhere and shoot anything, including, in the fifties, most of the stills emanating from movie sets and locations. One might press lightly against this convention, but no one wished to abandon it completely.

Not now. Not with everything else that was going on. This included, most significantly, television's replacement of the movies as the dominant form of mass entertainment in the United States. It also encompassed the emergence of a self-conscious and largely autonomous youth culture, once rock and roll had established itself as not just a sound, but a defining principle of adolescence. As a result of the play of these forces, media managers in their commercial calculations, began the process of redefining the relationship between celebrities and their audience, a continuing, ever-growing activity that now almost daily presents us with new astonishments.

Indeed, the kinds of pictures Sid Avery and his colleagues were encouraged to take in this period were, as I implied earlier, part of a strategy (or was it just more wishful thinking?) by which the movies, the press, and even obstreperous television itself—concerned with its ever-anxious middle-class market—attempted to blunt and deflect these radical changes.

The first of these changes, the decline of the movies and the rise of television, can be defined by a few simple statistics. In the years between 1930 and 1945 Americans had, on average, bought about 80 million movie tickets every week and had devoted something like eighty cents out of every dollar they spent on spectator amusements to the movies. Even in 1946, the first full year of peace, the nation gave Hollywood unprecedented evidence of its devotion. In that year 90 million admissions were sold each week, and the industry's gross take for the twelve months came to almost $1.7 billion.

Thereafter, without warning—and almost precisely coincident with the beginning of the postwar boom, when virtually every other major American industry was recording steady advances in sales and profits—the movies found themselves on a seemingly irreversible downward spiral. Over the next decade movie attendance dropped by almost 50 percent, and although gross revenues (steadied by advances in ticket prices) declined only about 23 percent, profits dipped an alarming 74 percent. In 1958 total box office receipts fell below $1 billion for the first time since 1941 (at which depressed level they remained for another decade). In that same period the number of films produced in the United States declined by over one-third.

Many factors contributed to the destabilization of the American film industry in this period. Immediately after that last great year in 1946, a portion of the audience had begun drifting away from the movies. There were suddenly, in those early postwar days, so many other things, big and little, to tempt the discretionary dollar—new cars and new homes and new refrigerators on the one hand, ballpoint pens and LP records on the other—and so many things, big and little, to tempt the discretionary leisure hour—night school on the GI Bill or sex (people began to think they could at last afford to have children) on the one hand, a drive in the country on a tank of unrationed gas on the other.

Then, too, there were the consent agreements, settling a longstanding antitrust suit, which obliged the studios to divest themselves of their comfortably, comfortingly profitable theater chains in the 1950s. And the demoralizing blacklist of individuals suspected of Stalinist sympathies, which was the industry's chief response to the anti-Communist hysteria of the time, took its toll on Hollywood's confidence and sense of community. Moreover, the aging of the executives who had presided over the classic era of American film, not to mention the aging of the stars who had been crucial to their success, contributed to the general air of bewilderment with which the industry confronted this moment of radical change.

But still . . . moving images! Free! In the privacy of your own home! That was the killer. It was only after television networking began in 1948, and the sale of sets started rising exponentially (a million in 1949, 4 million the next year, 32 million in 1954), that movie attendance took an alarming drop; 27.5 million customers, more than a third of the previous year's number, deserted in 1950 alone, and movie theaters all over the country started shutting down. Over four thousand of them would close before the decade was over. Simply put: It was the movies' fate to absorb the impact of television before the rest of us knew what hit us. It would reshape them before it reshaped our popular culture and our inner lives as well.

It is obvious that Sid Avery's pictures accurately reflect this moment when power in the image industry was so rapidly and radically realigned. Close to half the photographs collected here are of individuals the *Post* and the other magazines were interested in because of their work for television. It is interesting to observe, however, that very few of his subjects were people whose claim on our attention was first asserted in the new medium. There is James Garner, of course, the cool, sly, stylish star of *Maverick*, epitomizing the manner time would eventually teach us wore best in a medium where more intense personalities quickly wore out their welcome. There is Steve McQueen, who made his first indelible mark in TV's *Wanted: Dead or Alive* late in this decade. There is the then virtually unknown host of *Carson's Cellar*, working out of a cramped little TV studio in downtown Hollywood. These images of Johnny Carson are among the most fascinating in the book, for one searches them for clues to the strange power that has, since 1962, given him his apparently unchallengeable mastery of our midnights.

But for the most part these performers were television exceptions. So is another class of performer, composed of the truly great ones—exemplified here by Jack Benny. His delicious comic persona (that of a miserly coward) and his hold on the audience were, if anything, enhanced when he moved from radio to television, where we could see as well as hear his exquisitely timed reactions to misfortune. But most of the great radio names, like most of the truly great movie names who tried to make the transition to television, were not wildly successful. The dominant figures in the new medium in its early stages tended to be performers who achieved their first recognition elsewhere, drifted into television principally because they had nowhere else to go, and perhaps astonished themselves as much as anyone by what they achieved in it.

Among those Avery photographed, the most familiar to us now, of course, are those icons of the era, the people who virtually invented the sit-com as we know it, Lucille Ball and Desi Arnaz. *I Love Lucy* was not the longest-running television comedy (though it is certainly the longest rerunning half-hour in the medium's history), but their success with it enabled Ball (whose movie career had been second tier) and Arnaz (a sometime band leader whose movie career never was) to buy the RKO lot on which Ball had toiled with only modest success as a young actress, rename it Desilu, and convert it to TV production. But there were other transitions that were equally amazing at the time. Take, for example, Jackie Cooper, one of the most gifted child actors of the 1930s, happily reviving his career as an aging juvenile on two TV series—and going on from there to a solid career directing and producing in the new medium. Or Eve Arden, achieving authentic stardom as *Our Miss Brooks* (which was a Desilu show) after an endless apprenticeship in movies and radio. Or the veteran Ed Wynn, for whom TV revived his almost forgotten Broadway, vaudeville, and radio stardom, permitting him to make the final transition to the moment in which Avery caught him—as an Academy Award–nominated character actor in the movies.

On the other hand—and it is a hand heavily weighted with evidence of fifties television's primitivism—here is Danny Thomas, a deeply unfunny comedian, whose *Make Room for Daddy* (the show was later retitled so as to feature his name) somehow granted him a curious belovedness as well as his long-dreamed-of stardom. Here is Lawrence Welk and his moldy fig orchestra, rescued by the new medium from the endless road that had wound through the Eagles Club ballrooms of a hundred midwestern cities, acquiring ownership of Saturday-night television.

In the largest sense, then, it makes no difference how we look back on these figures: with increased regard for their historical significance, with the forgiving warmth of nostalgia, or with the contempt that the middle- and high-brow communities visited on them at the time still intact. For this fact remains inescapable: Television was essentially a haven for mediocre performers, people who had never threatened or discomfited anyone with great gifts and fitted easily, unambitiously, into its cramped confines.

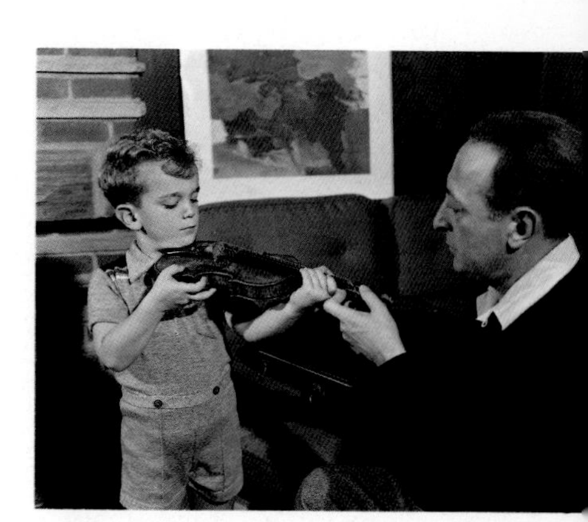

Another way of putting the point is that 1950s television, technological miracle though it certainly seemed to us, was not by any stretch of the imagination the movies as we had known them. The new medium simply did not have the scope, the glamour, the practiced facility, dramatic and otherwise, that the older medium had. Therefore the movie industry's leadership perhaps could be forgiven its halting response

to its competitor, its sense that anything that generally looked this hasty, tinny, and . . . well . . . second-rate must quickly decline of its own ineptitude once its novelty wore off.

Talk about wishful thinking! Not to mention naïveté. And yet, of course, it cannot be said that the moguls' response to a technological revolution that was about to trigger a social revolution was without precedent. Something like it has been customary on the part of those most directly affected by every major technological innovation in a century in which history has been irresistibly shaped by inventions of television's scope—from the automobile and the airplane to the computer.

Everyone knows what the old Hollywood finally did to counter television; how the studios, now needing to make fewer films, began phasing out, quite early in the fifties, long-term contracts for actors, writers, and directors, cutting back their rosters of full-time employees in craft, technical, and support departments, virtually ceasing to make program features, the kind of genre films that had in the past routinely supported everyone's movie habit. Everyone knows, too, that the marginal studios of poverty row (practitioners of the lowest level of genre filmmaking) simply failed, as did the careers of those marginal stars who did

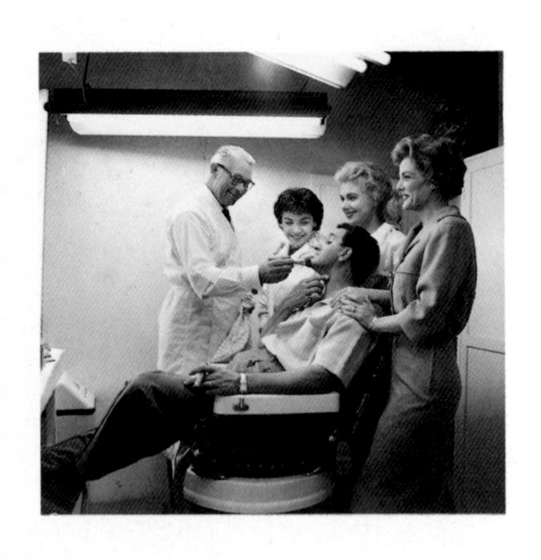

not accompany the genres over to television, where detective stories, westerns, and family comedies found new prosperity as weekly series. We also know that the studios counter-programmed against television with the big-screen processes, with increased production in color, with epic and spectacular films grander in scale than anything TV could offer, and that some of these films did manage briefly to reassemble the old mass audience in the theaters, becoming the largest-grossing films of the fifties. On the other hand, it soon became clear that such pictures failed about as often as they succeeded and that this mode of production was not something prudent, nervous executives could live with day in, day out.

As the decade wore on, in short, it became more and more obvious that the entire lower end of the demographic scale was lost to television, that it would be lured back to the movies only occasionally, essentially unpredictably. At the same time it began to seem that all was not lost. Two groups were proving themselves surprisingly faithful to film. One was, of course, the adolescent audience, whose need for a place to go on dates where they were free of prying parental eyes remained as strong as ever. The other was an older, more self-consciously serious crowd, beginning to learn that movies were an "art." This group, the product in part of the postwar boom in higher education, scornful of the conventions of genre and old-fashioned star acting, was looking for something more "realistic" in content and manner: movies that took up what they regarded as substantive issues and ideas in a sober fashion. In other words, films were beginning to attract that curiously schizophrenic audience—half teenagers, half middle-brows—that remains to this day essential to the prosperity of the industry.

More so than previously, more so than now, the two major components of that audience shared a common (indeed, overriding) anxiety. It was about finding, establishing, and defending their place in the world; that is to say, balancing personal need, the assertion of one's integrity as an individual, against the imperatives of the several communities to which everyone owes some measure of allegiance—namely, family, corporation, and government. This is, of course, the central issue of adolescence in every era of modern times. It is much less often an issue as pressing for adults as it was in the fifties, when concern over it became the distinguishing characteristic of popular culture.

As Peter Biskind has observed in *Seeing Is Believing*, the best book about American film of the fifties, the movies came at this issue (actually it was a set of interrelated issues) from every possible angle—left, right, and centrist; both directly and in all kinds of metaphorical guises—science fiction, westerns, crime dramas, war films; enlisting all manner of authority figures—generals and lawmen, scientists and doctors, even an architect or two to help us sort things out. Psychiatrists, who had been played almost exclusively as comic figures in prewar movies, became, in postwar film, great, solemn setters-to-right, with members of what we were learning to call "the helping professions"—an understanding social worker, a wise and patient teacher—often providing an explanatory chorus or two. (Even Hitchcock, under pressure from the censors no doubt, employed a shrink to provide a notably lame and dramatically ludicrous explanation of Norman Bates's lunacy in *Psycho*.) Generally, these figures affected some sort of compromise between individual and community needs. As Biskind demonstrates, they were always building a consensus or repairing one, pretty much the way Eisenhower was doing in the White House most of this decade, pretty much the way executive committees in both the private and the public sectors were doing.

There were a few irredeemable tragedies,

of course— among them the knothead Prewitt (Montgomery Clift) in *From Here to Eternity*, the psychopathically angry screenwriter, Dix Steele (Humphrey Bogart), in *In a Lonely Place*, the sweetly self-destructive Plato (Sal Mineo) in *Rebel Without a Cause*. But we were given to understand that their sad fates were the direct result of their inability to find and join the vital center. There were also throwbacks to a more rugged kind of individualism, like Sheriff Will Kane (Gary Cooper), unable to break the pacifist consensus in *High Noon*, defending his pusillanimous fellow townsmen against the gunslingers who threaten their smug peace anyway, then riding off in disgust. But they were the exceptions. Even the era's immortal delinquents—Dean in *Rebel Without a Cause* and *East of Eden*, Brando in *The Wild One* and most especially *On the Waterfront* (where he actually moves from minor thuggishness to leadership of the new reformist consensus on the racketeer-ridden docks), Sidney Poitier in *The Blackboard Jungle*—end up feeling Much Better, on their way to Useful Citizenship, thanks to interventionist therapy of one kind or another. As for adults, sweet reason, sometimes rather forcefully stated, always wins out: Henry Fonda turns around the jury bent on falsely convicting (largely on racist grounds) an Hispanic youth accused of murder in *Twelve Angry Men;* Gregory Peck turns down the big job in broadcasting in order to spend more time with his emotionally needy family in *The Man in the Gray Flannel Suit* but stumbles into a sweet little real estate deal anyway; William Holden imposes his idealism on an *Executive Suite*, wins the presidency of the company, yet retains the loyalty of the wife he has been neglecting for his work.

And so on and on. Why were we so determined that everything should come out all right for us in our little bourgeois worlds? Was the great world that scary? Were we that frightened of the Bomb? Of the Russians? Of McCarthyism? Of rock and roll? It is beyond the scope of this essay to say. What we can say is that when the movies ceased trying to be all things to all men, when they surrendered the genres, which had assured their acceptance at every age and social level, to television or adapted them to the specific needs of young people and the culturally aspiring but socially and intellectually nervous middle class, they found their salvation. Maybe they no longer bestrode popular culture, but they had found their safe niche. That, in the process, the movies lost their old romantic élan, the giddy vitality, the often surreal disjunctions between

reality as we experienced it and reality as it was presented on the screen in former times, was of small concern to the industry. It was actually applauded by critics who had been trying for years to sober up the movies and hold them accountable to earnest, middle-class cultural standards. Put it another way: The movies, like a good fifties movie hero, had finally joined the only consensus that counts in America. And, like him, they became, for the most part, tedious bores. The medium's period of adjustment was, aesthetically speaking, its historical lowpoint.

I make no claims for Sid Avery as a conscious social and cultural critic, aware of all this as he was making his pictures of Hollywood people in the 1950s. That was not his job—and the social commentators whose job it was were not doing it with great acuity at the time, either. I do, however, make large claims for the photographer's instincts and wit. He had a gift for getting at the truth behind the public images of his subjects. The tentativeness he finds in James Dean, for instance, cuts through the cultish silliness that has accreted around him over the years. The freckled freshness Avery finds in Kim Novak, so at odds with the bland enigma of her screen image, is revelatory in the same way. Similarly, the sweetness and vulnerability in his portrayals of Steve McQueen, for instance, seem to me to reveal the essence of his appeal in a way that many of his screen roles did not.

Avery's work with Brando is even more arresting. The portrait of him with bongos and African mask, a hint of reserve (or withdrawal from the publicizing process), seems to me more

than a great portrait of an actor; it seems to me a portrait of the generation whose inarticulate aspirations he summarized. And the accompanying shot of the actor tidying up his little rented house in Beverly Glen—what a wonderful comment that is. Older people were always telling Brando he had to clean up his act, and here he was doing exactly that. The pictures of Paul Newman and Joanne Woodward early in their film careers have a similar resonance. The modesty of their accommodations, their rejection of anything that smacks of "Hollywood," speak for all the deeply seri-

ous young performers of their day, trained in some variation or other of the Stanislavsky method, determined not to "sell out" (what a fifties phrase that is!) to fame and fortune, representing a new force that would redefine stardom as an institution.

In these pictures it seems to me Avery is stripping away self-consciousness. Or perhaps he is revealing a redefinition of that quality by the younger Hollywood generation. In any event, they provide a wonderful contrast to the satirical edge we find in some of his other photographs. For there are moments when gentle, kindly Sid Avery insists on parodying the pieties of an age— and approaches the country claimed by Diane Arbus. I love, for example, the not-quite-natural crook of Frankie Laine's arm as, armored in tail fins, he waves goodbye to his family and sets off to work; the de trop balloons—nobody is entitled to this much happiness—afloat over Sammy Cahn and family as they splash in their swimming pool; the too perfect serenity in Bogart's den. Shouldn't one dog be scratching fleas? Shouldn't the kid be squirming just a little? Then, too, there is the bizarrely lit religious statuary in Danny Thomas's backyard and the regimental alignment of his family before it; the disconcerting cracks in Jackie Cooper's driveway; the mad glitter in George Jessel's eye. They all dislocate us, in some way overturn our expectations about these famous, favored lives.

None more so, now, than the pictures of Rock Hudson and his friends. Talk about miming! All were enlisted in the effort to propagate

the fiction of youthful ordinariness—garden-variety heterosexuality—that was imposed on this rather sad figure as a condition of his stardom. It is not just the knowledge of his true nature that the passage of time has granted us, not just our acceptance of homosexuality as a way of being that is not to be judged or pitied, that makes these images seem so obviously posed. They *are* posed. They openly signal that fact, openly yet sympathetically signal a subtext subverting their ostensible meaning. They have, therefore, a poignancy and a capacity to make us reflect on a vanished time and place that is quite extraordinary.

So it is with all of Sid Avery's work. The magazines for which he worked have all disappeared—victims of the very forces that inform many of his images. Most of the people he portrayed have passed on or have drifted into the enigmatic realm of nostalgia. The Hollywood that he covered has changed almost beyond recognition. But his pictures are, finally, a surprisingly rich metaphor that forces us to contemplate not merely the popular culture of three and four decades ago, but the values—the middle-class consensus, if you will—that informed and was informed by what we saw and heard in the mass media. For some of us his photographs force a confrontation with a past that (not always usefully) continues to inform our thoughts and our reveries. For others they will, perhaps, summon up the thought contained in L. P. Hartley's famous epigram: "The past is a foreign country. They do things differently there." But however you approach these pictures, you will find in them an insinuatingly artless art. And many haunting resonances.

Richard Schickel

Hollywood
AT HOME

Tennessee Ernie Ford with his wife, Betty, and their two sons, Jeffrey and Brion, boating near their "Long Valley Ranch" in Clear Lake, California (1957).

F*unny Papers: Ernest Borgnine* (above) *with his wife, Rhoda, and daughter Nancy.*

OPPOSITE *Ernest Borgnine in his North Hollywood bungalow the year he won his Oscar for* Marty *(1955).*

Fond Farewells: Singer Frankie Laine is waved off to work by his wife, Nan Grey, and their two children (1957).

Wild Goose at Roost: Frankie Laine at home with his wife, Nan Grey (1954).

Shelley Winters (opposite) *and her husband Vittorio Gassman (1952).*

XXCENTVRY
ITALIAN ART
ENGLISH
Italian

D*ebbie Reynolds on her way to the set of* The Pleasure of His Company.

Debbie Reynolds (opposite) *takes part in some family fun with son, Todd, and daughter, Carrie (1960).*

Bing Crosby with son Harry and momentarily distracted daughter, Mary Francis (1961).

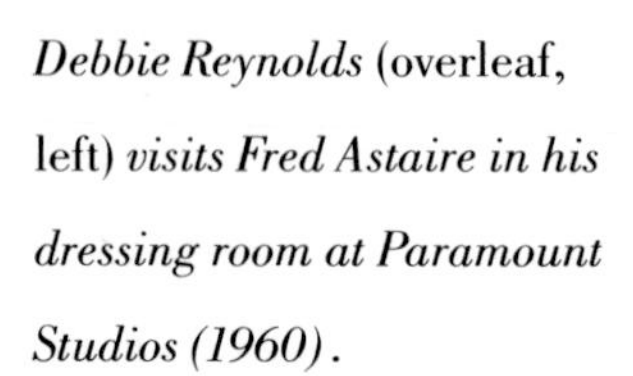

Debbie Reynolds (overleaf, left) *visits Fred Astaire in his dressing room at Paramount Studios (1960).*

Jack Benny (overleaf, right) *and* Post *writer Peter Martin at Republic Studios. Benny, with his exquisitely timed reactions to misfortune, was one of the few radio stars who made a graceful transition to television (1957).*

FRED

PROD. DEPT.

Git-gat-gittle": Danny Kaye (opposite) *tries out one of the comedy songs his wife, Sylvia Kaye, wrote for him as their daughter, Dena, joins in.* ABOVE *Danny Kaye in the locker room of the Hillcrest Country Club golf course (1958).*

D*anny Thomas* (above) *performs at a Christmas benefit in Los Angeles.*
OPPOSITE *Danny Thomas and wife, Rosemarie, with their children, Theresa, Marlo, and Tony (1958).*

I*da Lupino* (opposite) *and husband Howard Duff at home (1957).*

Jack Palance (above) *at home with his wife, Virginia, and their two daughters, Holly, who is now an actress herself, and Brooke (1954).*

A*udrey Hepburn* (above) *and husband Mel Ferrer play outside their Los Angeles home.*

OPPOSITE *Audrey Hepburn on her bike at Paramount (1957).*

Marx-a-Kart

Former child star Jackie Cooper with his wife, Barbara, and children Julie and Christina. Cooper continued acting as an adult but also became a director and producer (1961).

Joanne Woodward and Paul Newman (above) *on the set of* Rally 'Round the Flag, Boys!

OPPOSITE *Domestic Duties: Paul Newman and Joanne Woodward, Beverly Hills (1958).*

Domestic Bliss: Newman and Woodward at home (1958).

Composer Sammy Cahn (above) *seeks further inspiration beneath some visible symbols of his success.*

OPPOSITE *High Hopes: Sammy Cahn, his wife, Gloria, their children, Stephen and Lori, and a friend in the pool of their Los Angeles home (1959).*

Producer Stanley Kramer, famous for his "literate" films, shares the secret of his success with his son (1954).

The Douglas Family Incognito: Kirk, his second wife, Anne, and their two sons, Peter Vincent and Eric Anthony, Beverly Hills (1962).

Eve Arden (above), *her husband, Brooks West, and her two daughters, Elizabeth and Constance.* OPPOSITE *Arden with sons Douglas and Duncan in the year she achieved stardom in TV's* Our Miss Brooks *(1956).*

The Photographer Photographed: James Garner (above) *shoots for the family album.* RIGHT *A Gentle* Maverick*: James Garner with wife Lois Clark, stepdaughter Kimberly Clark Garner, and baby daughter Greta (1959).*

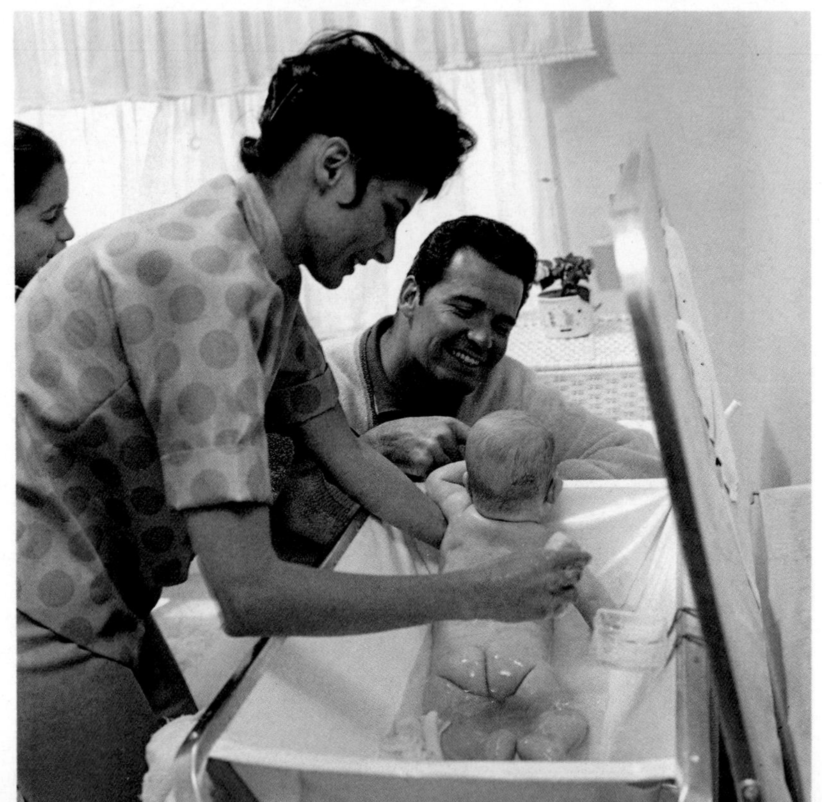

On the Move: Their son Steven bids farewell to Humphrey Bogart, Lauren Bacall, and their Jaguar XK 120. OVERLEAF, LEFT *On the Waves: Bogart at the helm of his beloved* Santana. OVERLEAF, RIGHT *Bogart and Steven study a model of* Santana *(1952).*

The Bogarts at home. The boxers who arranged themselves so photogenically were named Harvey, George, and Baby.

Steve McQueen (opposite) *belies his tough screen image car-ing for his daughter, Terry.* ABOVE *Steve McQueen with wife, Neile, and daughter, Terry (1960).*

Steve McQueen shows off his Jaguar SK-SS to John Sturges, director of The Great Escape, *on the Goldwyn lot in Hollywood (1960).*

9 STAGES 8

Dean Martin ostentatiously avoiding temptation (1961).

Martin takes a break during a television show taping (1961).

Dean Martin doting on his daughter as his wife, Jeanne, and the other girls peer on. His son makes mischief with the photographer (1961).

T*he Rat Pack (and associate members) on the set of* Ocean's Eleven *(1960)*.

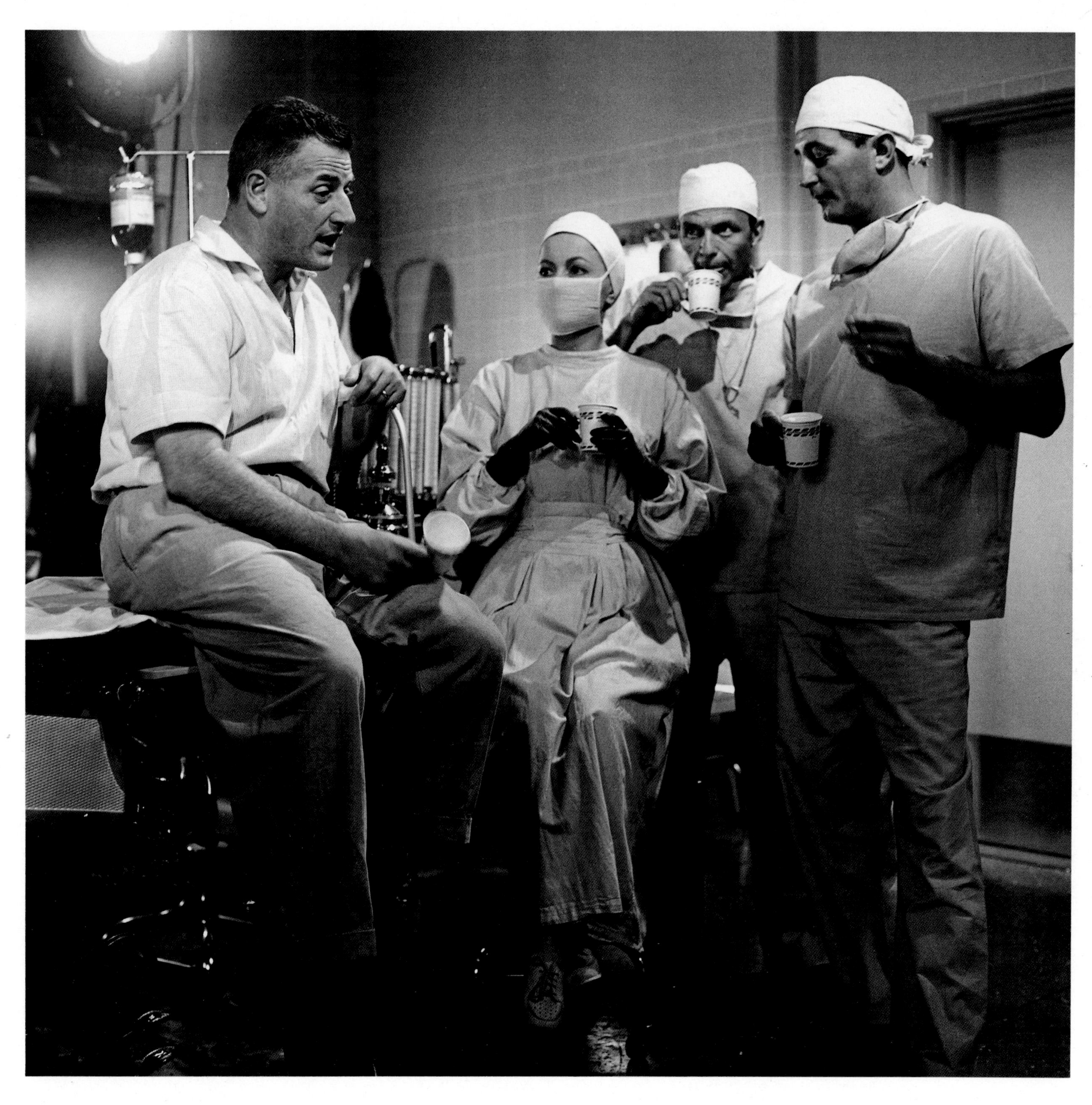

Stanley Kramer on the set of Not as a Stranger *with Olivia de Havilland, Frank Sinatra, and Robert Mitchum. It was the first film Kramer directed (1954).*

Sammy Davis, Jr., in the den of his Hollywood Hills home (1960).

Sammy Davis, Jr., and his wife Laray White Davis at the premiere of* Can Can*; leaning forward is leading Hollywood photographer Nat Dillinger (1960).*

Mamie Van Doren and her Big Band trumpet player Ray Anthony strike a rather obvious pose (1957).

Dolls: Tuesday Weld studies some cut-outs fashioned in her own image (1960).

Johnny Carson at work on his first TV show, Carson's Cellar *in Los Angeles (1953)*

Sports Buff: Comedian Joe E. Brown on the UCLA sidelines (1955).

Sportsman: Joe E. Brown with his wife, Kathryn, after a dip in the pool at his Brentwood home (1951).

R*ock Hudson* (above) *working out at his North Hollywood Hills home*. OPPOSITE *Rock Hudson looking larger than life (1952)*.

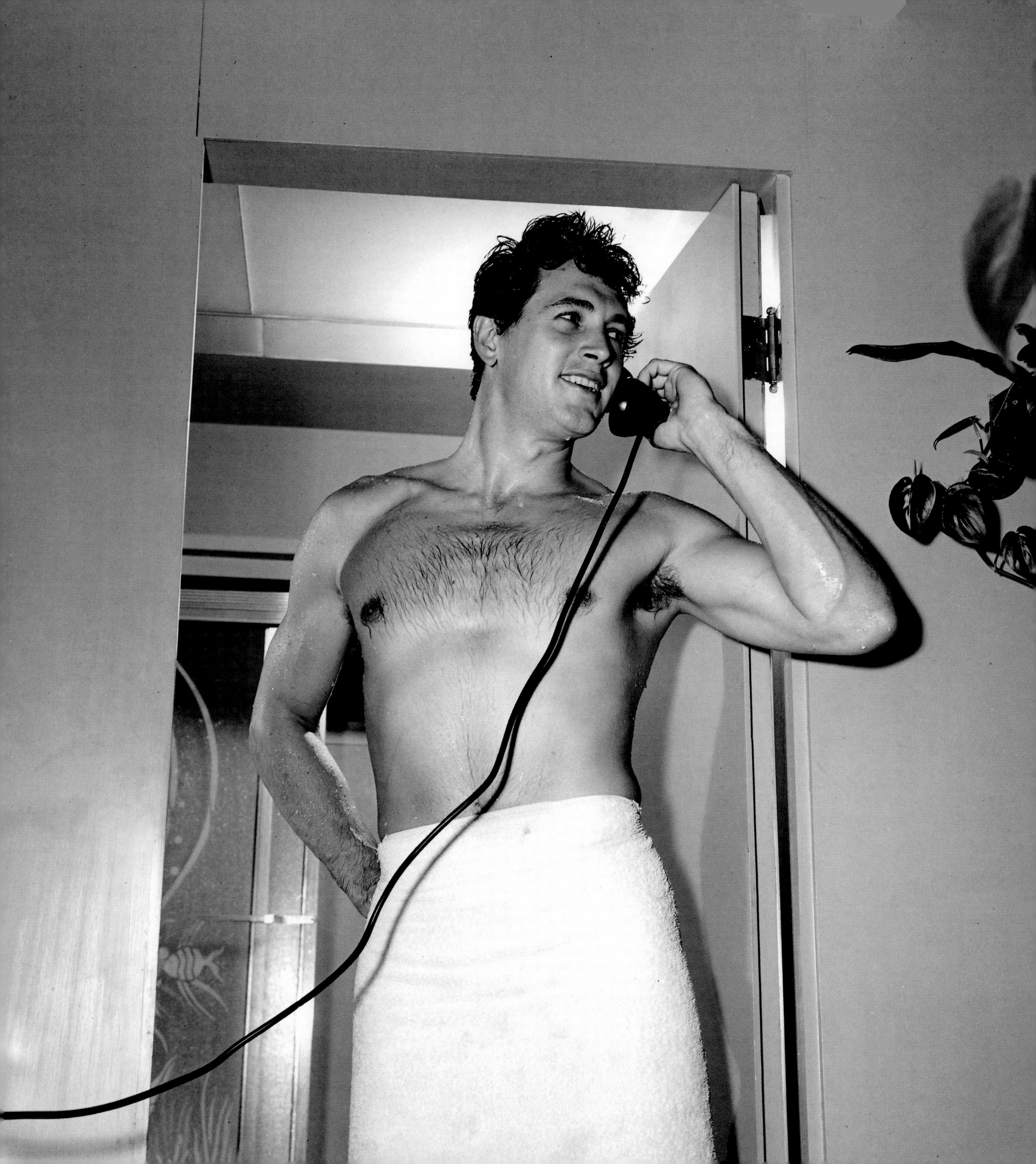

Rock Hudson (above) *entertains his Hollywood friends at home—a friendly game of charades.* OPPOSITE *Rock serves barbecue to actor Bob Preble, script girl Betty Abbott, actress Julia Adams and her husband, Leonard Stern, and actress Lorie Nelson. Photograph taken for a Saturday Evening Post article, "How To Create a Movie Star" (1952).*

A WOLF
N CHEF'S
LOTHING

Inger Stevens (1963).

Kim Novak (1952).

Kim Novak demonstrates the range of her pensivity (1952).

Starlet Elaine Stewart gets the star treatment in the MGM Stills Studio (1953).

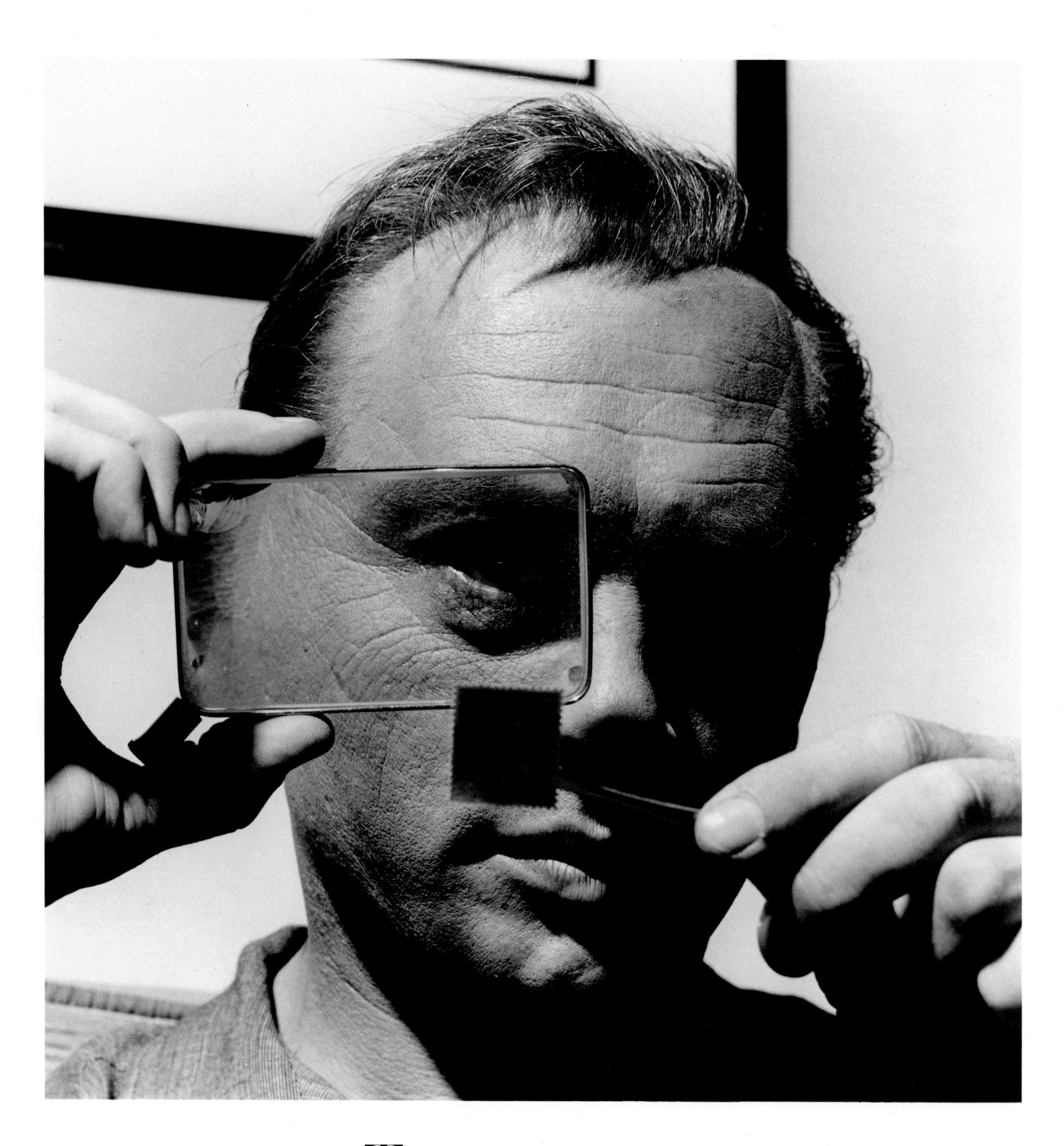

The stamp collector, a.k.a. Yul Brynner (1958).

B*rynner contemplates a prop knife from his film* The King and I *(1958)*.

Dalton Trumbo *(above) surrounded by his pre-Columbian art. He began collecting when he was blacklisted for alleged Communist affiliations and was living in Mexico. He won an Oscar writing under a pseudonym in 1957 and returned to Hollywood and was writing under his own name (*Spartacus, Exodus*) when this picture was taken in 1961.*

OPPOSITE *Celebrity lawyer Jerry Geisler at his office desk flanked by pictures of his two idols, Clarence Darrow and Earl Rogers (1959).*

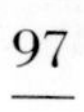

L*onely Tony Perkins*" (above) *was the title of the article this photograph illustrated (1959)*.

OPPOSITE *An Actress Prepares: Joanne Woodward studies a script (1958)*.

T*he Perfect Fool." Ed Wynn* (above) *in makeup.* OPPOSITE *Ed Wynn during a rehearsal break while making the film* The Diary of Anne Frank. *Actor Gary Merrill is in the background (1959).*

G*lenn Ford* (above) *with family dog*. OPPOSITE *Glenn Ford on the set of* The Sheepman *(1958)*.

The many moods of Marlon Brando (1955).

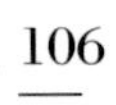

SOUPS
HONEY
GRAHAMS

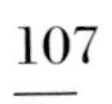

Clark Gable at home in Encino, California (1957).

Elizabeth Taylor catches the sun on the Giant *set (1955).*

James Dean: Portraits of the rebel (1955).

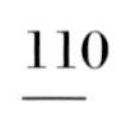

James Dean (opposite) *photographed on the set of* Rebel Without a Cause *(1955).*

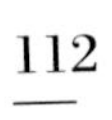

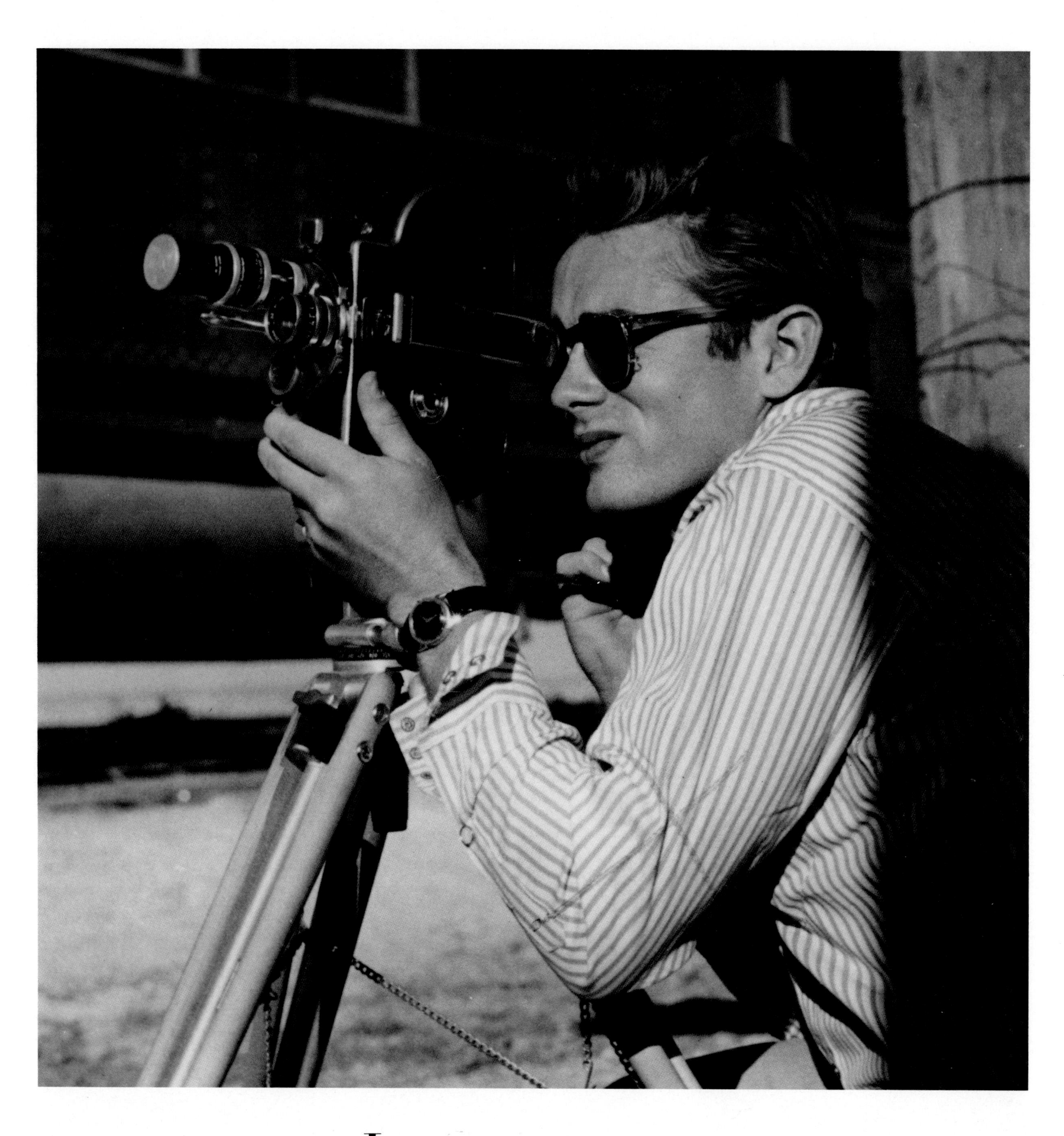

James Dean on the Marfa, Texas, set of Giant *(1955).*

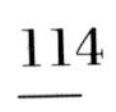

At Ease: The post-presidential Dwight D. Eisenhower (opposite) *grills steaks and potatoes at his Palm Springs home (1961).*

ABOVE *Odd Couple I: Rossano Brazzi and Jimmy Durante meet over the backfence they shared (1958).*

P*erfect Couple: Brazzi with sometime costar Sophia Loren* (above) *at his Beverly Hills home.*
OPPOSITE *Odd Couple II: Brazzi with his wife, Lydia, at a party in their Hollywood home. Mitzi Gaynor and her husband, Jack Bean, are in the foreground (1958).*

Anthony Perkins and Janet Leigh talk to Steve McQueen, visiting them on the set of Psycho *(1959)*.

Ed Wynn views rushes of The Diary of Anne Frank *with Millie Perkins and director George Stevens, who called Wynn "the best actor of our time" (1959).*

Shirley MacLaine during the taping of the CBS Shower of Stars *(1955)*.

Guy *Madison, star of the television series* Wild Bill Hickock, *entertains guests at his Los Angeles home.*
Rory Calhoun of Wells Fargo *is seated on the right (1953).*

Glenn Ford (above) *discusses a scene from* The Sheepman *with Shirley MacLaine and director George Marshall (1958).*

OPPOSITE *Elizabeth Taylor, Montgomery Clift, and director Edward Dmytryk prepare a scene for* Raintree County *(1956).*

GEN

We All Loved Lucy: The great comedienne clowns on the set of her immortal TV show (1956).

Parks: Lawrence Welk and guests at the annual Lawrence Welk picnic (1957).

Perks: *Welk and his band pose with cars donated by his TV sponsor, the Chrysler Corporation (1958).*

Business agent Bo Ross with one of his many Hollywood clients, Fred MacMurray, outside the Polar-Pantry, one of MacMurray's investments (1951).

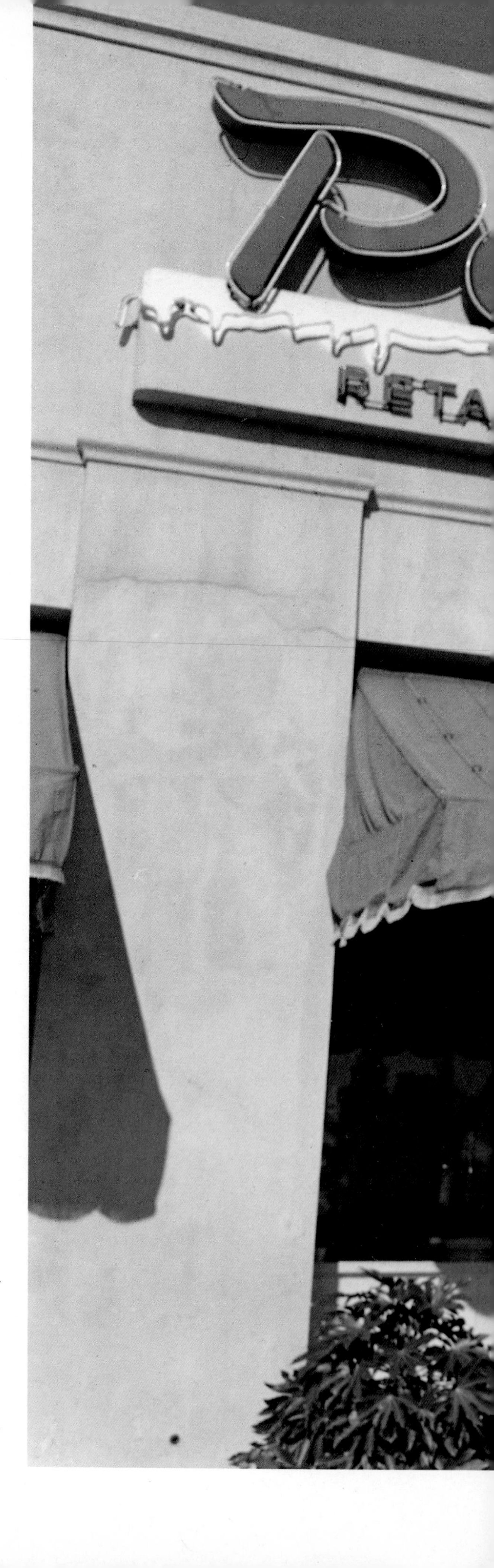

lar-Pantry
MEATS
ICE CREAM

Bob Newhart as *World's Greatest Hurdler (1961).*

Bob Newhart keeping up with current affairs in his suite at the Beverly Hills Hotel (1961).

Zsa Zsa Gabor shows off her "pet purse" in the dressing room of her Bel Air home (1958).

George Jessel breakfasting at his Santa Monica home. The self-styled Toastmaster General of the United States, he claimed never to have eaten lunch or dinner at home (1953).

The famous comedians' table at the Hillcrest Country Club. Left to right *Groucho Marx, George Jessel, Milton Berle, Eddie Cantor, and Buddy Lester. The comics met for lunch there every day (1953).*

Out On the Town: (left to right) *Humphrey Bogart, Lauren Bacall, Danny Thomas, George Jessel, and Phil Silvers (1953)*.

Jack Linkletter interviews Ronald and Nancy Reagan at the Hollywood premiere of Sayonara *(1957).*

Director George Stevens and his son George Stevens, Jr., at the Hollywood premiere of his movie Shane *(1953).*

Dean Martin attacked by autograph hounds (1961).

Jayne Mansfield signs autographs in front of Dino's restaurant on the Sunset Strip in Los Angeles (1961).

Liberace on *Art Linkletter's* House Party *(1956)*.

Nat "King" Cole performs at Ciro's Night Club. In the audience Jack Palance and Gig Young (1954).

143

Red Skelton rests backstage before appearing on CBS's Shower of Stars *(1955).*

ABOUT THE AUTHORS

SID AVERY has been an award-winning photographer for almost fifty years. His early photo-essays appeared in many magazines, among them the *Saturday Evening Post*, *Look*, and *Colliers*. His work is in the permanent collections of the Metropolitan Museum of Art, New York's Museum of Modern Art, and the Los Angeles County Museum; and in the private collections of Andy Warhol, Bruce Weber, and Ronald and Nancy Reagan. In the last twenty years Mr. Avery has run his own television commercial production company and has been ranked among the top television commercial directors in the world. He is also the founder of the Motion Picture and Television Photo Archive, which makes available some of the finest of the classic Hollywood photographs. *Masters of Starlight* contained pictures from an archive of which Mr. Avery was the principal founder. He lives in Los Angeles with his wife, Diana.

RICHARD SCHICKEL has reviewed movies for *Time* magazine since 1972; before that he was *Life*'s film critic. He is the author of many books, notably *The Disney Version*, *His Picture in the Papers*, *D.W. Griffith: An American Life*, *Intimate Strangers: The Culture of Celebrity*, and *Schickel on Film*, a collection of essays. He is at work on a book about American movies during World War Two. Mr. Schickel has held a Guggenheim Fellowship and has won the British Film Institute book prize. He is also a producer-writer-director of television documentaries.